MIDDLE EAST LEADERS™

OSAMA BIN LADEN

Suzanne J. Murdico

rosen
central™

The Rosen Publishing Group, Inc.,
New York

For Vinnie

Published in 2004 by The Rosen Publishing Group, Inc.
29 East 21st Street, New York, NY 10010

Library of Congress Cataloging-in-Publication Data

Murdico, Suzanne J.
Osama bin Laden/by Suzanne J. Murdico.— 1st ed.
     p. cm. — (Middle East leaders)
Summary: Examines the life and leadership skills of Osama bin Laden, whose terrorist network, Al Qaeda, is believed to be responsible for terrorist attacks on people and buildings around the world.
Includes bibliographical references and index.
ISBN 0-8239-4467-0
1. Bin Laden, Osama, 1957– 2. September 11 Terrorist Attacks, 2001. 3. Terrorism—United States. 4. War on Terrorism, 2001–
[1. Bin Laden, Osama, 1957– 2. Terrorists. 3. September 11 Terrorist Attacks, 2001. 4. Terrorism. 5. War on Terrorism, 2001–]
I. Title. II. Series.
HV6430.B55M87 2003
958.104'6'092—dc22

2003011568

Manufactured in the United States of America

104
apple

CONTENTS

■ Osama bin Laden is the financier of Al Qaeda, a worldwide terrorist organization. He is shown here in a frame capture from a videotape released after the September 11, 2001, attacks on the United States.

Those who lived through the events of September 11, 2001, will never forget that day. It was a day that not only changed America but also had a profound impact around the world. Although it began as a typical late summer day in the northeastern United States, September 11 soon turned into a tragic day. The worst terrorist attack ever committed on American soil was to occur.

In an extremely well-coordinated attack, nineteen terrorists hijacked four American jetliners. All four planes were scheduled for cross-country trips—two from Boston to Los Angeles, one from Washington, D.C., to Los Angeles, and one from Newark, New Jersey, to San Francisco. To make these long trips, the jets were loaded with thousands of gallons of highly flammable jet fuel. The terrorists had managed to smuggle small box cutters past airport security. They used these weapons to take control of the planes from the pilots. The terrorists then turned the jets into deadly missiles.

When all was said and done, more than 3,000 people had lost their lives and many more had been injured. New York City had lost two of its most famous landmarks. The Pentagon near Washington, D.C., was shown to be vulnerable. And passengers in Pennsylvania died helping thwart another suicide attack. American citizens became acutely aware that the United States was open to terrorist attacks. And everyone who watched the dramatic events unfold in person or on live television would always remember that day.

Following the initial shock and sadness of the events of September 11, 2001, many questions haunted people around the globe. Who was responsible for these attacks? Who had the tremendous power, wealth, and cunning to carry them out? The mastermind behind these acts of terrorism had to have the ability to plan and coordinate multiple strikes. This person needed followers so committed to a cause that they were willing to

FBI TEN MOST WANTED FUGITIVE

MURDER OF U.S. NATIONALS OUTSIDE THE UNITED STATES;
CONSPIRACY TO MURDER U.S. NATIONALS OUTSIDE THE UNITED STATES;
ATTACK ON A FEDERAL FACILITY RESULTING IN DEATH

USAMA BIN LADEN

Date of Photograph Unknown

Aliases: Usama Bin Muhammad Bin Ladin, Shaykh Usama Bin Ladin, the Prince, the Emir, Abu Abdallah, Mujahid Shaykh, Hajj, the Director

DESCRIPTION

Date of Birth:	1957	**Hair:**	Brown
Place of Birth:	Saudi Arabia	**Eyes:**	Brown
Height:	6' 4" to 6' 6"	**Complexion:**	Olive
Weight:	Approximately 160 pounds	**Sex:**	Male
Build:	Thin	**Nationality:**	Saudi Arabian
Occupation(s):	Unknown		
Remarks:	He is the leader of a terrorist organization known as Al-Qaeda "The Base." He walks with a cane.		

CAUTION

USAMA BIN LADEN IS WANTED IN CONNECTION WITH THE AUGUST 7, 1998, BOMBINGS OF THE UNITED STATES EMBASSIES IN DAR ES SALAAM, TANZANIA AND NAIROBI, KENYA. THESE ATTACKS KILLED OVER 200 PEOPLE.

CONSIDERED ARMED AND EXTREMELY DANGEROUS

IF YOU HAVE ANY INFORMATION CONCERNING THIS PERSON, PLEASE CONTACT YOUR LOCAL FBI OFFICE OR THE NEAREST U.S. EMBASSY OR CONSULATE.

REWARD

The United States Government is offering a reward of up to $5 million for information leading directly to the apprehension or conviction of Usama Bin Laden.

■ Osama bin Laden became the chief suspect following the 1998 bombing of United States embassies in Dar es Salaam, Tanzania, and Nairobi, Kenya. The Federal Bureau of Investigation distributed this wanted poster for bin Laden, making him one of the FBI's most wanted criminals in the world.

die for it. But who hated the people of the United States enough to commit these deadly acts?

At the Federal Bureau of Investigation (FBI), one possible suspect came immediately to mind. He had previously declared war on America. He was a suspect in several other terrorist attacks against Americans. He had been on the FBI's Ten Most Wanted Fugitives list since 1999. His name was Osama bin Laden.

CHAPTER ONE

WHO IS OSAMA BIN LADEN?

■ During the later 1990s, all that was known of bin Laden's whereabouts was that he was somewhere in Taliban-controlled Afghanistan. Occasionally, he could be seen in a video, speaking against the United States or warning of a coming attack.

Before September 11, 2001, the majority of Americans were unfamiliar with the name Osama bin Laden. After the terrorist attacks, however, they had many questions about him. In some ways, bin Laden is a man of mystery. At the very least, he's a man of many contradictions.

Physically, Osama bin Laden is almost frail looking. He's quite tall—about six feet five inches—and so thin that he is gaunt. He often walks with the aid of a cane and appears older than he actually is. By many accounts, he is soft-spoken and perhaps even shy. Despite his fragile appearance and gentle manner, however, bin Laden clearly has a commanding presence. He comes from an extremely wealthy family, yet he has spent many years living in mountain caves. While he now openly hates all things American, he was once an ally of the United States.

In photos, bin Laden is often shown holding an AK-47 assault rifle, yet he seems less than comfortable with it. To his many followers, he is viewed as a war hero. Stories of Osama bin Laden's feats on the battlefield become more legendary with each retelling. Yet disbelievers have questioned whether bin Laden ever actually fought on the front lines. They say that his help in war efforts really came from the sidelines in the form of money and organizational skills.

So how do we unravel the mysteries to find the truth about Osama bin Laden? To better understand how he evolved into the man he is today, we need to learn about his past. His family background and upbringing helped him establish his interest in the Islamic faith. His education and time spent working in the family business ignited his religious passion and helped him develop his skills. And the point at which he developed an intense hatred for America came later, with turmoil and war in the Middle East.

A Wealthy Family

Osama bin Laden was born in Saudi Arabia in 1957. He is the seventeenth son of fifty-two children born to Mohammed bin Awad bin Laden. The bin Ladens are Muslims, which means that they follow the faith of Islam. Muslim men are allowed to have four wives at the same time. Mohammed bin Laden kept four wives at a time, then divorced one wife to marry another.

Each of Mohammed bin Laden's wives had several children, who formed tight-knit clans. While most of Mohammed bin Laden's wives were from Saudi Arabia or Egypt, Osama bin Laden's mother was from Syria. She had no more children after Osama. Despite the fact that he had so many siblings, Osama grew up somewhat isolated from them.

Osama's Father

The rags-to-riches story of Osama bin Laden's father is the stuff of legend. The story goes that the elder bin Laden, who was born in Yemen, immigrated to Saudi Arabia on foot when he was a teenager. He could not read or write, and he worked as a bricklayer. For this he earned little money.

Legend has it that Mohammed bin Laden was working on a construction project for Abdul Aziz, the king of Saudi Arabia. The king saw bin Laden's design ideas and was very impressed. He gave Mohammed bin Laden important construction contracts for work on the royal palace. Later, the king awarded bin Laden's company with contracts to renovate the holy cities of Mecca and Medina. This was an incredible honor for a Muslim.

Over time, these royal contracts helped Mohammed bin Laden turn his small bricklaying business into a $5 billion a year construction company. It was called the Saudi bin Laden Group.

Mohammed bin Laden was killed in a plane crash in 1967. His son Osama was just ten years old. After his father's death, Osama bin Laden inherited an estimated $250 million. This amount was his share of the family fortune. Later, he would use this money to help fund his terrorism campaign against the United States.

Young Adulthood

Many of bin Laden's brothers and sisters chose to travel, live, and study outside the Middle East. Some attended college in Europe and others in the United States. One of Osama's brothers even studied at the prestigious Harvard University in Massachusetts. Osama, however, had no desire to leave Saudi Arabia. He decided to study management and economics at King Abdul Aziz University in Jedda. One of his professors—Sheikh Abdullah Azzam—greatly influenced bin Laden. Azzam was a Muslim fundamentalist who followed a very strict interpretation of Islam. He believed that Islamic lands should be freed of all foreign influences.

Osama bin Laden graduated from the university in 1979. Afterward, he spent some time working for his family's construction business. During that period, the company was rebuilding holy mosques in Mecca and Medina. This experience served to increase bin Laden's passion for Islam. Over time, this passion would evolve into extremist views of the Islamic faith. Eventually, these beliefs would motivate bin Laden to take action by fighting in a holy war.

COUNTRY CAPSULE: Saudi Arabia

Capital

Riyadh

Total Area

756,985 square miles (1,960,582 sq km) (slightly more than one-fifth the size of the United States)

Border Countries

Jordan, Iraq, Kuwait, Qatar, United Arab Emirates, Oman, Yemen

Population

22 million

Religions

Sunni Muslim 90 percent; Shia Muslim 10 percent

Language

Arabic

Literacy Rate

63 percent

Occupations

Services 63 percent; industry 25 percent; agriculture 12 percent

Imports

Machinery and equipment, foodstuffs, chemicals, automobiles, textiles

Exports

Oil and oil products

Natural Resources

Oil, natural gas, iron ore, gold, copper

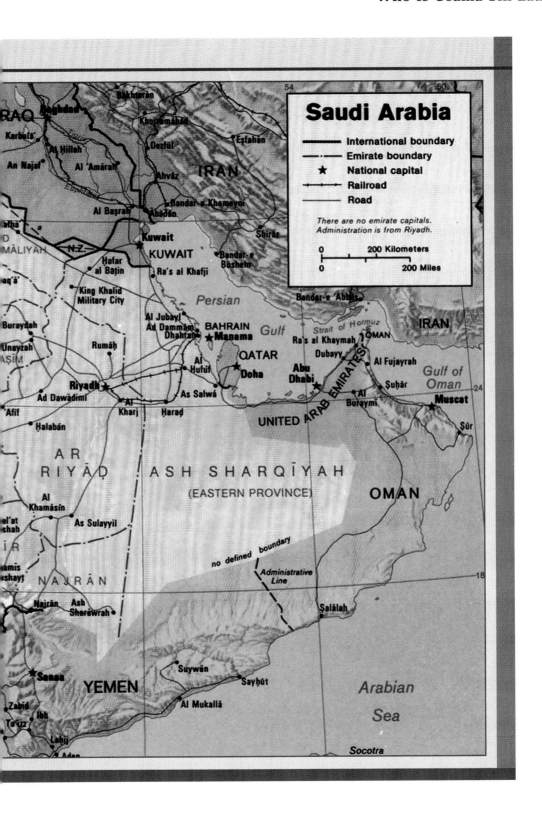

Some reporters have written that Osama bin Laden was a playboy during his young adulthood. They say that he often traveled to Beirut, which at the time was known for its wild nightlife. Bin Laden was said to enjoy indulging in alcohol and women. It has even been reported that he was involved in some drunken bar fights. If these stories are true, this behavior would be contrary to his strict Islamic beliefs. Some reporters dispute these stories, though, saying that they simply never happened. It's known that several of bin Laden's half brothers did enjoy this type of decadent lifestyle. So it's possible that their stories have been mixed up with Osama's.

Islam

Islam is one of the major religions in the world. The prophet Muhammad, an Arab born in Mecca, started Islam in the seventh century AD. Followers of Islam are called Muslims. *Islam* is an Arabic word meaning "surrender to the will of Allah [God]," and *Muslim* means "one who surrenders [to Allah]." While the beginning of Islam was among Arabs, modern-day countries with the largest Muslim populations include Indonesia,

■ Islam's most holy religious site, the Grand Mosque in Mecca, Saudi Arabia, draws thousands of worshipers for daily prayers. Each year, the mosque hosts pilgrimages of Muslim faithful from around the world, whose duty it is to travel to Mecca at least once.

Pakistan, India, Iran, Bangladesh, and Turkey. However, Arab states such as Saudi Arabia, Egypt, Syria, and Iraq still boast the highest percentages of population who are Muslim.

Muslims regard several places in the Middle East as holy ground. The three most sacred cities of Islam are Mecca, Medina, and Jerusalem. Mecca and Medina are in modern-day Saudi Arabia. Jerusalem is in modern-day Israel.

- Mecca is the holiest city for Muslims because it's the birthplace of Muhammad. An important event for all Muslims is to make a pilgrimage to Mecca at least once in their lifetime. Whenever they pray, Muslims face Mecca.
- Medina is the second holiest city. After being driven out of Mecca, Muhammad fled to Medina and was welcomed there. Medina is also home to Muhammad's burial site.
- Jerusalem is the third holiest city because a Muslim shrine called the Dome of the Rock is found there. Muslims believe that this site is where Muhammad ascended to heaven to receive Allah's commandments.

■ A second holy site revered by Muslims is the mosque at Medina, also in Saudi Arabia. Here lies entombed the prophet Muhammad, who devoted the last forty years of his life to preaching the words of Allah.

Islamic Beliefs

Muslims believe that Allah revealed what is known as the Divine Word to Muhammad. These revelations were recorded in the Koran—the Muslim holy book. Similar to the Bible in some ways, the Koran forbids lying, stealing, adultery, and murder. It teaches virtues such as kindness, honesty, and charity. It condemns impatience and cruelty. Muslims submit to Allah by performing the main duties defined in the Five Pillars of Faith:

- Profession of faith—To become a Muslim, a person must profess the belief that there is only one God and that Muhammad was a prophet of God.
- Prayer—Muslims pray five times each day: at sunrise, at noon, in the afternoon, at sundown, and in the evening. On Fridays, Muslims gather to pray at a mosque, or Muslim house of worship.
- Fasting—During Ramadan (the ninth month in the Muslim year), Muslims are forbidden to eat or drink between dawn and dusk. At the end of Ramadan, they have a

■ Iraqi children study the Koran at a mosque in Baghdad. Like most Muslim children, Osama bin Laden also received religious instruction from a young age. Later, as a teenager, bin Laden would begin to use more radical interpretations of the Koran to direct his life.

three-day celebration called Festival of the Breaking of the Fast.

- Charity—Muslims believe that it's important to help the poor. In some Muslim countries, citizens are required to pay a *zakat*, which is a donation to the needy.
- Pilgrimage—At least once during their lifetime if they are able, all Muslims are required to make a pilgrimage to Mecca, known as the hajj. This pilgrimage is a four-day journey that retraces the path of Abraham.

A Modest Lifestyle

Not a great deal is known about Osama bin Laden's personal life. And some of the information that has been reported is doubtful at best. One main reason is that bin Laden generally avoids answering questions about his personal life. Another reason is that the facts are difficult to verify because bin Laden has been in hiding for so long. We do know, however, that he has four wives and many children, and lives a modest lifestyle.

Bin Laden married his first wife, a Syrian woman who was a relative, when he was just seventeen years old. He later married two other women—both from Saudi Arabia—and had fifteen children with his three wives. In 2000, the forty-something-year-old bin Laden married his fourth wife. She was a seventeen-year-old girl from Yemen. Bin Laden has even used marriage for political gain. He married off one of his daughters to a powerful political ally. Also, his eldest son is married to the daughter of one of bin Laden's lieutenants.

Even before Osama bin Laden went into hiding and began living in caves, he rejected modern luxuries. Instead, he chose a simpler lifestyle. Many of his relatives lived in expensive mansions in Saudi Arabia. Although he could easily afford this type of home, bin Laden and his wives and children lived in modest houses. It has been reported that the houses were not even equipped with air-conditioning despite the extreme heat. "I don't want to get used to the good life," bin Laden told a journalist. This aspect of bin Laden's personality makes his followers admire him all the more. They see a millionaire who has sacrificed his wealth to live a humble life, much like their own. They see a man whom they would follow into battle against "the infidels." Among his followers, Osama bin Laden is viewed as a true believer in the faith of Islam.

CHAPTER TWO

THE MAKING OF A TERRORIST

■ The Soviet invasion of Afghanistan in 1979 angered millions of Muslims around the world. Bin Laden volunteered his time and money to help the Afghans defeat the mighty superpower. Here, Soviet tanks travel a road to Kabul with Afghan onlookers.

Two major events became turning points in the life of Osama bin Laden and led him down the path to terrorism. The first event was the Soviet invasion of Afghanistan in 1979. The second was the first Persian

Gulf War in 1991. Both events involved the United States's presence in the Middle East, which bin Laden actively fought against.

Soviet Invasion

On December 26, 1979, the Soviet Union invaded the Central Asian country of Afghanistan. The Soviet Union was a Communist country. Soviet troops were sent to support a new Communist government in Afghanistan. Because the Soviets did not follow Islam, many Muslims felt that they should not be in Afghanistan. They viewed the Soviet Union as a godless power that had attacked their Muslim brothers.

Mujahideen

At the time of the Soviet invasion, Osama bin Laden was twenty-two years old. Like thousands of other Muslims, he volunteered to go to Afghanistan to fight the invading troops. With money he had inherited from his family's construction company, bin Laden began organizing a campaign to defeat the Soviets. He also raised additional funds from wealthy Arabs. Bin Laden used the money to pay for food, weapons, and medical care. He also flew in construction equipment to help build roads and tunnels. In addition, he established training camps for the Muslim fighters. These Afghan resistance fighters were known as the mujahideen, or "holy warriors."

Like the mujahideen, the United States was also opposed to the Soviet Union's invasion of Afghanistan. The U.S. government wanted to curb the spread of Communism. To this end, the United States helped the Muslim fighters by supplying them with money and

COUNTRY CAPSULE: Afghanistan

Capital

Kabul

Total Area

251,739 square miles (652,001 sq km) (slightly smaller than the state of Texas)

Border Countries

Turkmenistan, Uzbekistan, Tajikistan, China, Pakistan, Iran

Population

27.5 million

Religions

Sunni Muslim 84 percent; Shia Muslim 15 percent; other 1 percent

Languages

Afghan Persian 50 percent; Pashtu 35 percent; Turkic languages 11 percent; 30 other languages 4 percent

Literacy Rate

31.5 percent

Occupations

Agriculture 68 percent; industry 16 percent; services 16 percent

Imports

Food and petroleum products, most consumer goods

Exports

Hand-woven rugs, cotton, wool, animal pelts, precious and semiprecious gems

Natural Resources

Oil, natural gas, coal, minerals, salt, precious and semiprecious stones

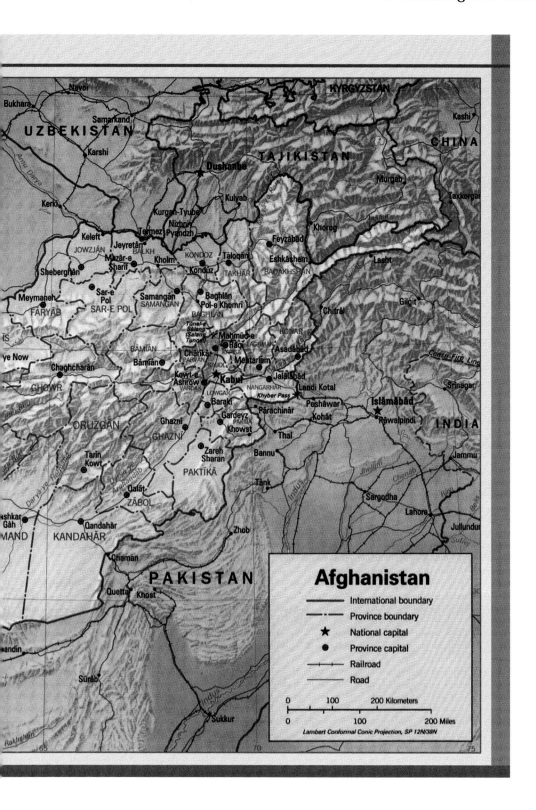

weapons. For a time, the United States and Osama bin Laden were actually fighting on the same side.

Jalalabad

The Soviet invasion of Afghanistan lasted for ten years, finally coming to an end in 1989. The final battle was a particularly fierce one in a town called Jalalabad. According to some accounts, Osama bin Laden fought in the front lines at Jalalabad and several other battles. After that final encounter, the Soviet troops retreated and left Afghanistan.

The victory against the Soviets was especially sweet for Osama bin Laden. With its huge numbers of troops and military might, the Soviet Union was considered by many to be an invincible superpower. But the rebel mujahideen had managed to force its withdrawal from Afghanistan. Of course, they did have a considerable amount of help from the United States and other countries opposed to Communism.

Government Opponent

After the war with the Soviet Union, bin Laden was honored as a hero in both Afghanistan and Saudi Arabia.

■ Mujahideen freedom fighters lived in the Afghan mountains for ten years fighting the Soviets. Their weapons and supplies often came from the United States, through Osama bin Laden's organization to assist the mujahideen.

He returned to his homeland and resumed working for the family's construction company, the Saudi bin Laden Group. Soon, though, bin Laden became a vocal opponent of the Saudi royal family. He openly criticized the Saudi government's policies regarding the United States. Despite the U.S. government's support against the Soviet invasion in Afghanistan, bin Laden didn't think the United States had any business being in the Middle East. He viewed America's presence there as an affront to Muslim independence.

Persian Gulf War

Osama bin Laden's criticism of both the Saudi government and the United States grew even stronger during the first Persian Gulf War. On August 2, 1990, Iraq invaded its tiny neighboring country of Kuwait. This invasion led to the first Persian Gulf War. Although there were several reasons for the Iraqi invasion, one of the most important was to acquire Kuwait's vast oil resources.

After gaining control over Kuwait, Iraq began moving troops to Kuwait's border with Saudi Arabia. These actions caused concern that Saudi Arabia would be the next target of an Iraqi invasion. Many industrialized nations around the world rely heavily on Kuwait and Saudi Arabia for their oil supply. These nations, including the United States, sent troops to Saudi Arabia to protect it from being attacked.

Once again, the presence of U.S. troops in the area outraged Osama bin Laden. In his eyes, the actions of the United States were for purely self-serving reasons— to protect its oil interests in Kuwait and Saudi Arabia. Bin Laden was also convinced that U.S. troops would

■ Iraq's invasion of Kuwait in 1990 brought the wrath of the world upon Iraq. The United States led a coalition of armed forces to push Iraq out of its southern neighbor in 1991. Shown here are Kuwaiti oil fields, set afire by retreating Iraqi troops.

stay in Saudi Arabia even after the war was over. He strongly opposed the Saudi government's decision to allow U.S. troops in Saudi Arabia. Because the holiest Muslim sites are located there, bin Laden considered the U.S. presence to be a violation of Muslim holy ground.

Becoming an Outcast

Osama bin Laden's outspoken criticism of the Saudi government caused the government to strike back. It threatened to destroy the bin Laden family construction

COUNTRY CAPSULE: Kuwait

Capital

Kuwait City

Total Area

6,880 square miles (17,819 sq km) (slightly smaller than the state of New Jersey)

Border Countries

Iraq, Saudi Arabia

Population

Nearly 2 million

Religions

Sunni Muslim 45 percent; Shia Muslim 40 percent; other 15 percent

Languages

Arabic, English

Literacy Rate

78.6 percent

Occupations

Government and social services 50 percent; services 40 percent; industry and agriculture 10 percent

Imports

Food, construction materials, vehicles and parts, clothing

Exports

Oil and refined products, fertilizers

Natural Resources

Oil, natural gas, fish, shrimp

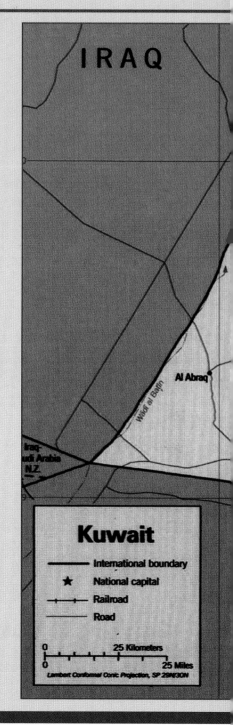

IRAQ

Al Abraq

Kuwait

———— International boundary

★ National capital

—•—•— Railroad

———— Road

0   25 Kilometers

0   25 Miles

Lambert Conformal Conic Projection, SP 29N30N

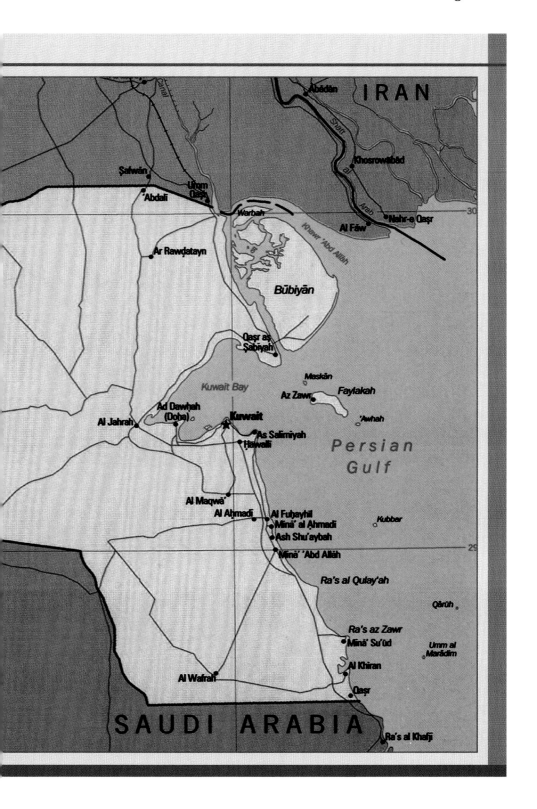

company. For a short time, the government put bin Laden under house arrest. Eventually, the pressure forced bin Laden to leave Saudi Arabia. He took his family, which by then included several wives and many children, and moved to Sudan.

Sudan is a poor country. A militant Islamic government was in power when bin Laden moved his family there. Bin Laden lived in Sudan from 1991 to 1996. He invested some of his inheritance in Sudan. He established a major construction company there. This made the Sudanese government accept him all the more.

Bin Laden's construction company built a major highway that connects the capital city of Khartoum with Port Sudan on the Red Sea. The highway has helped Sudanese business immensely. People respected bin Laden because he helped Muslims in his new country. Thousands of out-of-work Sudanese worked on the public project (and for other bin Laden companies). The highway became known locally as the Osama Road.

While building roads and helping other Sudanese infrastructure, bin Laden also began setting up terrorist training camps. These camps trained Islamic radicals from a number of countries. They also equipped the radicals to carry out terrorist acts. In 1996, the United States and Saudi Arabia pressured Sudan into expelling him from the country. Bin Laden then returned to Afghanistan, where he was welcomed back as a war hero and champion of Islam.

Saudi Exile

During the mid-1990s, Osama bin Laden also became an exile from his homeland of Saudi Arabia. By that

■ Sudan, in West Africa, welcomed Osama bin Laden after he left Saudi Arabia with his family in 1991. Bin Laden's investment in the construction company that built the highway shown here helped win him friends in the Sudanese government.

time, bin Laden's name was being linked to many terrorist activities, including the 1993 World Trade Center bombing. In 1994, Saudi Arabia revoked his citizenship and denied him access to his money and property within the country.

Breaking Family Ties

The same year that Osama bin Laden was exiled from Saudi Arabia, his family disowned him. They disapprove

Osama bin Laden

■ This tannery was partly owned by bin Laden. The Sudanese government gave bin Laden a share in the company as payment for road construction in the country. Bin Laden is said to have sold off all his Sudanese assets upon leaving for Afghanistan in 1996.

of his religious fanaticism, his extreme anti-American views, and his terrorist activities. The bin Laden family has publicly cut all ties with Osama.

Many Americans probably didn't know that several bin Laden family members were living in the United States before September 11, 2001. One of Osama's brothers was a lawyer in Boston. A nephew attended the University of New Hampshire. The Saudi bin Laden Group even donated $2 million to Harvard University.

After the September 11 terrorist attacks, the bin Laden family publicly condemned Osama's actions. However, the FBI advised the family members living in the United States that their safety was at risk. They quickly left the country for fear of retaliation against them for Osama's actions.

CHAPTER THREE
ORGANIZING THE TROOPS

■ Former Afghan mujahideen became bin Laden's core group of Al Qaeda terrorist troops. The radical Muslim group turned its anger toward the United States and Western influence in the region with worldwide campaigns of terror and bombing.

In 1989, the Soviet Union finally withdrew its troops from Afghanistan. It had spent ten years fighting the mujahideen. This was a huge victory for the Afghan resistance fighters. To many Muslims, it proved that guerrilla warfare and Islamic dedication could defeat a much larger and better-equipped enemy.

The end of the Soviet invasion of Afghanistan was also the turning point in Osama bin Laden's life. During this time, he began building the terrorist network that would become known as Al Qaeda. In addition, the end of the war opened the door for bin Laden's return years later to Afghanistan. He would live freely under the protection of the country's new government—the Taliban.

Al Qaeda

Bin Laden had used his family's wealth to aid the mujahideen in their uprising against the Soviet invasion. His financial backing helped recruit Muslims from many countries to fight in the war. Bin Laden's role in the mujahideen's victory against the Soviet superpower made the Saudi millionaire a hero to Muslims around the world. After the Soviet forces withdrew, bin Laden started an organization to aid veterans of the Afghan conflict. From this organization, Al Qaeda was born.

Al Qaeda is Arabic for "the base." Members of Al Qaeda include former members of the mujahideen and other Muslim extremists. After bin Laden was pressured to leave Saudi Arabia in 1991, he moved to Sudan. There, he established the Al Qaeda headquarters. He then began launching a series of terrorist attacks against Americans.

Most of these terrorist acts were aimed at American interests overseas. These included an attack on American servicemen in Somalia in 1993 and the bombing of two U.S. embassies in Africa in 1998. One of these terrorist attacks, however, was on America soil. The Al Qaeda bombing of the World Trade Center in 1993 would turn out to be just a sign of the much more devastating events to follow on September 11, 2001.

Goals of Al Qaeda

Al Qaeda has several goals. All are based on extremist views of Islam and the Koran. One main goal is to rid all Muslim countries of Americans and Western influence. Most important of these Muslim countries is Saudi Arabia, home to two of Islam's holiest places. A second goal is to destroy the country of Israel and give the land to the Palestinians. A third Al Qaeda goal is to cause the collapse of all Middle Eastern governments that support the United States.

Al Qaeda's goals do not revolve around one specific conflict. Members from around the world can be recruited for a variety of purposes. They work within a network of local terrorist "cells" that operate independently of one another. This way, they have Al Qaeda's training and support, but it's difficult to trace each cell back to the organization.

A New Kind of Terrorism

Although Al Qaeda members follow a major religion, the organization is

■ Al Qaeda terrorist camps sprung up in the mountains outside Kabul and Jalalabad, Afghanistan, in the early 1990s. A U.S. military strike on the Zhawar Kili Al-Badr camp following the 1998 U.S. embassy bombings in Africa did little damage to Al Qaeda.

definitely a terrorist organization of the twenty-first century. Al Qaeda is very different from terrorist organizations of the past. Most previous terrorists were motivated by local concerns, such as fighting over territory or a nation trying to gain independence. Al Qaeda members, however, are united by their Muslim faith and their common goals for Islam.

Al Qaeda has no single location from which its operations begin. Rather, it's a global network whose members can be found in terrorist organizations in many countries. Some of these countries include Afghanistan, Pakistan, Somalia, Yemen, Algeria, and the Philippines. Kashmir (a region shared by Pakistan and India) is also used by Al Qaeda members to hide from authorities. Having so many members in so many locations has enabled Al Qaeda to plan and carry out large-scale terrorist attacks like those of September 11, 2001.

Other important elements in carrying out its attacks are lengthy preparation and extremely careful planning. Terrorist acts linked to bin Laden and Al Qaeda were sometimes planned for several years. These include not only the September 11 attacks but also the 1998 bombings of two U.S. embassies in Africa and the attack on the USS *Cole* in 2000.

Al Qaeda also takes full advantage of twenty-first century methods of communication and transportation. For example, Al Qaeda members who executed the September 11 attacks communicated with one another through e-mail, faxes, and cell phones. Although Osama bin Laden is believed to live in caves, he reportedly uses a private jet to move him and his family from one location to another.

■ Members of the radical Muslim organization Hezbollah are shown here marching in an anti-Israeli rally in 1995. Experts believe bin Laden studied terrorist organizations like Hezbollah while he was establishing Al Qaeda in Afghanistan.

Links to Other Terrorist Groups

Experts believe that Osama bin Laden and Al Qaeda are at the center of an alliance of terrorist organizations. Al Qaeda is thought to have recruited Islamic radical groups from several Middle Eastern and North African countries. These groups are composed of Muslim fundamentalists whose views and goals are similar to those of Al Qaeda. They include Hezbollah in Iran and Lebanon, Al Jihad in Egypt, National Islamic Front in Sudan, and similar terrorist groups in Saudi Arabia, Indonesia, Morocco, Somalia, and Yemen.

■ After the Soviets left Afghanistan, Taliban rebels fought against the ruling government. Rebels shown here fight on the front line 8 miles (12.9 kilometers) from Kabul. Bin Laden's Al Qaeda organization began a partnership of sorts with the Taliban leaders.

The Taliban Rises to Power

In addition to Al Qaeda, Osama bin Laden has also been associated with the Taliban in Afghanistan. The Taliban, which means "religious students," ruled Afghanistan between 1996 and 2001. The group came into power following the ten-year war with the Soviet Union.

After the Soviet forces withdrew from Afghanistan in 1989, the Soviet-backed government remained in power. Soon, however, it began to lose ground to the mujahideen. In 1992, these rebel forces took control of Kabul, the country's capital. The existing government was overthrown, and a group of mujahideen members set up a new government. The various mujahideen groups did not work together, however, and began fighting one another. There was no central government, and a civil war broke out.

One of the mujahideen groups that had fought the Soviets was the Taliban. In 1994, they began to organize their members to form a unified force. They soon took over the city of Kandahar and then went on to capture Kabul in 1996. The Taliban became the ruling government of

■ The Taliban's takeover of Kabul and the Afghanistan government ended sixteen years of war. Pictured above is Darul Aman Palace in central Kabul, where the Soviet-backed government fell to Taliban fighters in 1996.

Afghanistan. After many years of war, the Taliban restored peace and order to the country. This peace came at a high price, however.

The Taliban followed a very strict interpretation of Islamic law. With this interpretation, all non-Islamic influences were banned from the country. These influences included movies, music, television, and art. Other rules included requiring all men to wear beards and banning all forms of entertainment, such as dancing or card playing. People who did not follow the rules risked severe punishment, such as beatings. Some were even executed for their "crimes." These executions were often performed as public displays. The Taliban used these public executions to instill fear in Afghan citizens and to keep them in line.

Islamic Fundamentalism

Not all Muslims agree with Osama bin Laden's views or Al Qaeda's goals. In fact, the majority of Muslims around the world don't support terrorism in any form. Islam is a religion that generally promotes kindness, charity, and nonviolence. So why does bin Laden organize terrorist activities in the name of Islam? Why do Al Qaeda members think that completing a suicide

Wahhabis

Like most religions, Islam has several divisions, or sects. The two main sects, started in the 600s, are Sunni and Shia. More than 80 percent of Muslims are Sunnis. They believe that Muslim leadership should be passed to those who are elected. The Shiites believe that the only rightful successors to Muhammad are descendants of Muhammad's son-in-law, Ali.

Among the Sunnis, several smaller sects arose. One of these sects, dominant in Saudi Arabia, is the Wahhabis. The Wahhabi sect is named for Mohammad ibn Abd al-Wahhab, an eighteenth-century reformer. Al-Wahhab believed that Islam had been corrupted after about 950. He taught that all Muslim beliefs and customs developed since that time were false and should not be followed. In an attempt to purify the Sunni sect, al-Wahhab opposed all practices not approved by the Koran. From al-Wahhab's and other conservative teachings arose Islamic fundamentalism.

mission against Americans will make them martyrs for the spiritual cause?

Osama bin Laden and his Al Qaeda followers are Islamic fundamentalists, or extremists. They believe in a very strict—and very old—interpretation of Islamic law as written in the Koran. In this extreme interpretation, it is the duty of all Muslims to attack a common enemy. In this case, the common enemy is anyone who does not follow Islam. Bin Laden and Al Qaeda members use this reasoning to justify violence against all non-Muslims. They also use it to justify suicide attacks. Because suicidal acts are generally forbidden under Islamic law, these kinds of attacks would normally not be allowed.

These types of extremist views are seen most often in poor Middle Eastern countries. Many people in these countries live in extreme poverty. They have few freedoms and often feel a sense of powerlessness. This may cause feelings of resentment against wealthy and powerful nations, such as the United States. These feelings may fuel hatred toward America and promote extremist views, along with terrorism.

■ The Taliban's strict rule forced women to give up their jobs. Female children could no longer attend school. Women were forced to wear the traditional burka *(above)* under penalty of public beatings or worse.

In a 1998 interview with *ABC News*, Osama bin Laden explained his feelings about terrorism. "In today's war, there are no morals," he said. "[Americans] rip us of our wealth and of our resources and of our oil. Our religion is under attack. They kill and murder our brothers. They compromise our honor and our dignity and dare we utter a single word of protest against the injustice, we are called terrorists."

Women and the Taliban

To Westerners, one of the most shocking and disturbing aspects of Taliban rule was the treatment of women. Girls were not allowed to attend school. Women were forbidden from working outside the home. Since the majority of teachers in Afghanistan had been women, many schools were closed. When outside the home, women had to be covered from head to toe, including their faces. They were not allowed outside the home without a male relative as chaperone. Women were also forbidden from wearing makeup and nail polish. Women who broke these rules were often beaten and sometimes even shot.

According to the Taliban, these rules were necessary to protect women and their honor. In their strict belief system, women and men who were not married had to be separated at all times to avoid temptation. A woman was not allowed to speak to any men except her husband and male relatives.

Sheltering bin Laden

After being expelled from both Saudi Arabia and Sudan, Osama bin Laden returned to Afghanistan. The Taliban was grateful for bin Laden's help in freeing the country

■ Hamza bin Laden *(center)*, the young son of Osama bin Laden, is shown reading a poem to Al Qaeda militiamen on November 5, 2001. Al Qaeda was preparing for attacks by United States military forces following the September 11 attacks.

from the Soviet Union. The group welcomed back the Saudi dissident and offered him political shelter in Afghanistan.

Soon, bin Laden became an important ally to the Taliban. He had a great deal in common with the group and its leader, Mullah Mohammed Omar. Both bin Laden and Mullah Omar hated the West, particularly America, and felt that it was a negative influence on Islam. The two men also shared a strict fundamentalist view of Islamic law.

O_{sama} b_{in} L_{aden}

■ Osama bin Laden is shown at al-Farouq training camp in Afghanistan during the summer of 2001. After the September 11 attacks, bin Laden continued to call for a holy war against America and other Western countries.

Bin Laden showed his support of the Taliban by donating some of his fortune to help it. In a display of unity, he also gave Mullah Omar one of his daughters to marry. In return, the Taliban let bin Laden live in Afghanistan. It also allowed him to set up training camps for terrorists. Although the U.S. government demanded that the Taliban turn over bin Laden, it refused. To give him up would also mean giving up his financial support.

Terrorist Training Camps

If not for the Taliban, Al Qaeda would most likely not exist today. The Taliban let bin Laden use Afghanistan as home base for his Al Qaeda network. From the country's deserts and caves, bin Laden and Al Qaeda operated terrorist training camps. They taught Muslim fundamentalists from countries around the world how to use terrorism to achieve their goals. They showed them how to wage a jihad, or holy war, against America and the rest of the non-Muslim world.

Over the years, thousands of terrorists, including several of the September 11 hijackers, were trained at these camps. Terrorists learned such skills as using small arms, building and detonating explosives, and committing acts of sabotage. They learned how to plan, coordinate, and carry out terrorist attacks. And they even learned ways to avoid drawing attention to themselves while living in America or Europe.

Training Al Qaeda terrorists who came from many different countries gave bin Laden a distinct advantage. He was able to organize attacks on Americans from several different fronts. To launch an attack on Americans in Yemen, for example, a Yemeni terrorist cell was used. The September 11 terrorists came from several different Muslim countries, including Saudi Arabia, Egypt, and the United Arab Emirates. Modern technology allows these distant cells to communicate easily with one another and plan their attacks.

CHAPTER FOUR

AT WAR WITH THE UNITED STATES

■ Osama bin Laden sits with his top lieutenant, Ayman al-Zawahiri, at a secretly located meeting of Al Qaeda in Afghanistan. Intelligence experts today believe al-Zawahiri managed the planning of the September 11 attacks on the United States.

The September 11 terrorist attacks were a clear declaration of war against the United States. But many people wondered why anyone would want to wage war with America. The attacks seemed to come out of the blue. What had Americans done to deserve such an assault? What most people didn't realize was that the seeds of this war had been growing for many years.

Although most Americans see their country as good and kind, not everyone throughout the world agrees with this view. In many Arab and Muslim nations, conservative Muslims criticize liberal American values. They believe that these values spread moral corruption throughout the world. They see Americans as materialistic—interested only in money and material objects, rather than in spiritual enlightenment. Many conservative Muslims disapprove of American exports, such as movies, music, and clothing. They believe that this Western influence will destroy traditional Islamic values and culture.

Osama bin Laden and other conservative Muslims also disagree with American foreign policy. "They don't see us as we see us," Jon B. Alterman, a Middle Eastern expert at the U.S. Institute of Peace, told the *New York Times Upfront*. "Overseas, we're seen as arrogant, we're seen as huddling behind the high walls of embassies, as supporting corrupt regimes, and as being utterly indifferent to Arab suffering."

While the events of September 11 may have come as a complete shock to the majority of Americans, there had been signs of trouble brewing. The worst terrorist attack in U.S. history had been foreshadowed in several similar yet smaller acts of terrorism against Americans overseas. The man thought to be behind all of these terrorist acts—Osama bin Laden—believes that terrorism is justified in the name of Islam.

■ United States military officers speak with a Saudi government official at the Al Kharj military base in Saudi Arabia. Attacks on American forces in Saudi Arabia in 1997 were blamed on Al Qaeda.

Why bin Laden Hates America

Osama bin Laden hates America, its government, and its citizens for several reasons. But two reasons in particular stand out. The first is that bin Laden opposes the stationing of U.S. troops in Saudi Arabia. The second reason is that he disagrees with the U.S. policy of support for Israel.

U.S. Troops in Saudi Arabia

Following the 1991 Persian Gulf War, U.S. troops remained in Saudi Arabia to help train the Saudi military. They were also there to protect the country from potential problems with Iraq. Their presence in Saudi Arabia infuriated bin Laden. Rather than viewing the U.S. troops as a helpful resource, he saw them as the enemy. To bin Laden, these non-Muslims on Muslim soil were infidels.

According to ancient Islamic tradition, there should "not be two religions in Arabia." In a 1997 interview with CNN, bin Laden said that the continued U.S. military presence in Saudi Arabia was an "occupation of the land of the holy places." Bin Laden and his followers believed that the Saudi government, not

COUNTRY CAPSULE: Israel

Capital

Jerusalem

Total Area

8,019 square miles (20,769 sq km) (slightly smaller than the state of New Jersey)

Border Countries

Lebanon, Syria, Jordan, Egypt, and the Palestinian territories of the West Bank and the Gaza Strip

Population

6 million

Religions

Jewish 80 percent; Muslim 15 percent; Christian 3 percent; other 2 percent

Languages

Hebrew, Arabic, English

Literacy Rate

95 percent

Occupations

Public services 31 percent; manufacturing 20 percent; finance and business 13 percent; commerce 13 percent; construction 7.5 percent; services 6.5 percent; other 9 percent

Imports

Raw materials, military equipment, investment goods, rough diamonds, fuels, consumer goods

Exports

Machinery and equipment, software, cut diamonds, chemicals, textiles and apparel, agricultural products

Natural Resources

Copper, phosphates, bromide, potash, clay, sand, sulfur, asphalt

American troops, should be responsible for defending the country.

U.S. Support of Israel

For many years, American support of Israel has been a source of conflict with Arab nations. In 1947, the United Nations voted to partition Palestine between Jews and Arabs so that the Jewish people would have a homeland. The following year, Israel declared its independence, sparking an attack by several Arab countries. During the ensuing war, many Palestinians took refuge in the Gaza Strip (controlled by Egypt) and the West Bank (which Jordan took over). Later, during a 1967 war, Israel occupied these areas, adding more territory to its borders. This displaced more Palestinians and further intensified the dispute between Israelis and Palestinians.

Although peace talks have been attempted many times, they have all failed. In recent years, the conflict between Israel and Palestine has grown stronger. Both sides have employed deadly force against each other. While Palestinians have used random shootings and suicide bombings, Israelis have used their mighty military forces. In some cases, the United States has supplied the weapons used by Israelis against Palestinians.

Israel is a democracy that has many of the same values as the United States and its European allies. The United States believes in religious freedom, and many Jews live and work in America. For these reasons, the U.S. government has supported Israel in its conflict with the Palestinians. This support, however, generates a great deal of anger among many Arabs, including Osama bin Laden. Because these Arabs side with the

■ Seen here is the Arrow anti-missile missile displayed in Tel Aviv, Israel. It was built jointly by the Israeli and United States governments. The close relationship of the two countries is one cause of tension in the Middle East.

Palestinians, they view the United States as being an ally of the enemy.

Declaration of Jihad

In Osama bin Laden's view, the United States is an enemy of Islam. For this reason, he has issued two fatwas against Americans. A fatwa is a religious decree issued by an Islamic leader. Bin Laden's fatwas were declarations of jihad, or holy war. In the first fatwa, issued in 1996, bin Laden called upon his followers to rid Muslim holy lands of all Americans and Jews. Regarding Americans, bin Laden was specifically referring to the U.S. troops stationed in Saudi Arabia.

In 1998, bin Laden's fatwa became more comprehensive and even more chilling. This time, he called for the death of all Americans. In an interview with John Miller of *ABC News*, bin Laden vowed to "send the bodies of American troops and civilians home in wooden boxes and coffins." He added, "We don't differentiate between those dressed in military uniforms and civilians. They are all targets in this fatwa."

Americans as Terrorists

As much as Americans believe that Osama bin Laden is a terrorist, bin Laden himself believes that Americans are the real terrorists. In his opinion, he and his followers are fighting a righteous war against American terrorism. According to bin Laden, American acts of terrorism include occupation of the Holy Land in Saudi Arabia. He also blames the United States for the starving of a million Iraqi children due to United Nations sanctions following the Persian Gulf War of 1991. He also suggests that the dropping of atomic

Al—Jazeera
Exclusive

خــــاص
بالجـــزيرة

أولى

أســـامـــة بـن لادن

■ Bin Laden is seen here from a videotape released November 3, 2001. In his statement, bin Laden appealed to the 1.2 billion Muslims around the world to join Al Qaeda in a holy war against "infidel" Christians and Jews.

bombs on Hiroshima and Nagasaki, Japan, at the end of World War II were American acts of terrorism.

After the September 11, 2001, terrorist attacks on America, Osama bin Laden appeared in a videotaped broadcast on Arabic television. In the video, he attempted to justify his reasons for terrorism against Americans: "Our terrorism is a good accepted terrorism because it's against America, it's for the purpose of defeating oppression so America would stop supporting Israel, who is killing our children."

Attacks Against Americans

Although Osama bin Laden rarely claims responsibility for terrorist attacks, he often praises those who carried them out. After the September 11 attacks, for example, bin Laden reportedly thanked almighty Allah and bowed before him. In addition to September 11, many other terrorist attacks against Americans have been linked to Osama bin Laden. These acts of terrorism date back at least to 1993 and probably even earlier.

World Trade Center

Years before terrorists destroyed the World Trade Center, the New York City landmark was the site of another terrorist attack. On February 26, 1993, a bomb exploded in the parking garage located below the towers. The explosion occurred on a Friday, when tens of thousands of workers occupied the building. It destroyed six floors of the parking garage, leaving a 150-foot-wide (45.7-meter) crater in its wake. Six people died in the blast, and more than 1,000 others were injured.

FBI agents determined that more than 1,000 pounds of explosives had been transported into the parking

■ The aftermath of the 1993 World Trade Center car bombing left a 150-foot-wide (45.7-m) hole in the parking garage beneath the trade center complex. Al Qaeda was blamed for the blast and Ramzi Yousef was convicted as the mastermind behind the bombing.

garage in a rental van. Investigators were able to trace the van through the rental agency, and they arrested several suspects. The suspects were later tried and convicted of the bombing. The mastermind behind this terrorist attack was a Pakistani named Ramzi Yousef.

The FBI discovered that Yousef chose the World Trade Center as a target because he was hoping that one tower would fall over onto the other tower. This disaster would have killed as many as 250,000 civilians. According to the FBI, Yousef thought that this "would bring the attention of the American people to the plight of the Palestinians and cause America to realize that continued support of Israel would result in what was in effect a war." At the time of his arrest, Ramzi Yousef was staying in Pakistan at a guesthouse paid for by Osama bin Laden.

U.S. Military in Somalia

In October 1993, U.S. military personnel were bringing food and other supplies to Somalia. The troops were sent there ten months earlier to help with the United Nations famine relief efforts. Local guerrillas shot down a U.S. military helicopter, killing eighteen American service-men. Some of the soldiers' bodies were dragged through the streets of Mogadishu. In 1996, bin Laden was charged with training those who took part in the attack. In a 1997 interview with CNN, bin Laden admitted that his followers were responsible for killing the servicemen.

U.S. Embassies in Africa

On August 7, 1990, U.S troops arrived in Saudi Arabia after Iraq invaded Kuwait, causing the start of the first

■ The United States Embassy building in Nairobi, Kenya, stands ruined after a truck bomb exploded outside the building. Al Qaeda was blamed for the terrorist act. Bin Laden denied the allegations.

Persian Gulf War. On August 7, 1998—exactly eight years later—two truck bombs exploded outside U.S. embassies in Africa. One was in Nairobi, Kenya, and the other in Dar es Salaam, Tanzania. In Nairobi, 213 people died, including 12 Americans, and thousands more were injured. In Dar es Salaam, 11 people were killed and nearly 100 injured.

Although Osama bin Laden denied responsibility for these attacks, investigators believed he was guilty. Statements made by Al Qaeda members and faxes sent by

Osama bin Laden

■ Osama bin Laden went "underground" in 1998 after the United States Justice Department charged him with the African embassy bombings. On May 29, 2001, four followers of bin Laden's were convicted of the 1998 bombings.

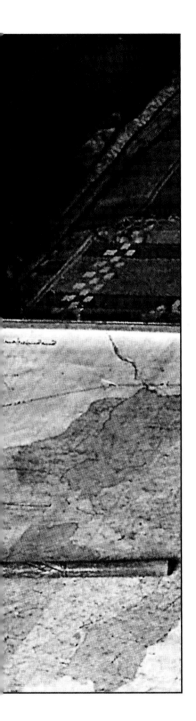

one of bin Laden's terrorist cells linked him to the attacks. In November 1998, the U.S. government charged bin Laden and several other suspects with the embassy bombings. When bin Laden could not be located, the U.S. government offered a $5 million reward for information leading to his arrest. In 1999, his name was added to the FBI's list of the Ten Most Wanted Fugitives. In May 2001, four people were convicted of the embassy bombings and received sentences of life in prison. All four were Al Qaeda members.

USS *Cole*

On October 12, 2000, the U.S. Navy battleship USS *Cole* was docked for refueling at the port of Aden in Yemen. Yemen is a small country near Saudi Arabia. A small boat loaded with explosives pulled up alongside the *Cole*, and two suicide bombers detonated the explosives. The blast created a 40-by-40-foot (12.2-by-12.2-m) gash in the side of the 505-foot (154-m) destroyer, killing seventeen sailors and injuring thirty-nine others.

Shortly before the *Cole* attack, Osama bin Laden had released a videotape. In it, he called for more violence in Yemen. Following the attack, five people suspected of planning it revealed that they had been trained in bin Laden's terrorist camps.

September 11, 2001

On the morning of September 11, 2001, millions of New Yorkers were just beginning their normal workday. But all sense of normalcy was about to end abruptly. At 8:47 AM, a jet plane crashed into the upper floors of the north tower of the World Trade Center. At 110 stories each, the twin towers were the second-tallest buildings in the United States and among the tallest skyscrapers in the world. The jet fuel ignited, and flames and dark clouds of smoke started to billow from the upper floors of the building. At first, many people assumed that the plane had been flying too low and had accidentally hit the skyscraper. Soon, however, they would find out that this was no accident.

As crowds of people watched the burning north tower, a second jet approached at a low altitude. At 9:02 AM, the onlookers stared in horror as the jet smashed into the side of the south tower. Now both towers were spewing smoke and flames as thousands of workers scrambled down flight after flight of stairs to escape the buildings. At the same time, hundreds of firefighters and police officers rushed to the scene to try to rescue those who were trapped inside.

Just when it seemed as though things couldn't get any worse, the unthinkable happened. At 9:50 AM—just forty-eight minutes after the south tower was hit—the massive structure collapsed in on itself and came crashing to the ground. The intense heat from the fires had melted the steel and concrete until they could no longer support

TIMELINE: September 11, 2001

8:47 AM American Airlines Flight 11, hijacked while en route from Boston to Los Angeles with ninety-two people on board, crashes into the north tower of the World Trade Center.

9:02 AM United Airlines Flight 175, hijacked while en route from Boston to Los Angeles with sixty-five people on board, crashes into the south tower of the World Trade Center.

9:21 AM All bridges and tunnels leading into New York City are closed.

9:26 AM For the first time in U.S. history, the Federal Aviation Administration orders all planes grounded and cancels all flights.

9:30 AM The New York Stock Exchange is closed.

9:41 AM American Airlines Flight 77, hijacked while en route from Washington, D.C., to Los Angeles with sixty-four people on board, crashes into the Pentagon.

9:48 AM The White House and the U.S. Capitol are evacuated.

9:50 AM The south tower of the World Trade Center collapses.

10:00 AM United Airlines Flight 93, hijacked while en route from Newark, New Jersey, to San Francisco with forty-five people on board, crashes into a field about eighty miles southeast of Pittsburgh, Pennsylvania.

10:13 AM The United Nations building in New York City is evacuated.

10:28 AM The north tower of the World Trade Center collapses.

10:45 AM All federal buildings in Washington, D.C., are evacuated.

11:00 AM New York City mayor Rudolph Giuliani orders the evacuation of lower Manhattan.

12:15 PM The U.S. borders with Canada and Mexico are closed.

the weight of the upper floors. Forty minutes later, the north tower collapsed, too. These great symbols of American wealth and success had taken several years and a great deal of money to build. Within a matter of seconds, they were reduced to smoldering heaps of rubble. Nearly 3,000 people, including 343 firefighters, lost their lives. And the world-famous New York City skyline would be forever changed.

Meanwhile, near Washington, D.C., a third hijacked jetliner was headed toward the Pentagon. The Pentagon is one of the largest office buildings in the world. It's the headquarters of the U.S. Defense Department and employs 23,000 military and civilian personnel.

At 9:41 AM, the jet plowed into the side of the five-story structure, creating a huge gaping hole. All 64 people on board the plane were killed, along with 125 workers inside the Pentagon. The side of the building that was hit had recently undergone renovations, and many workers had not yet returned to their offices. If they had, the death toll probably would have been much higher.

The fourth hijacked plane was the only jet that missed its intended

■ At 9:50 AM on Tuesday, September 11, 2001, the south tower of the World Trade Center collapsed. The nation was stricken with a sense of loss and outrage at the attacks on American soil by Al Qaeda.

target. Analysts believe that it was headed for a high-profile building in Washington, D.C.—most likely the White House or the U.S. Capitol. Fortunately, it never got there.

After four terrorists took control of the plane, passengers began making cell phone calls to their loved ones. The passengers were informed about the terrorist attacks at the World Trade Center and the Pentagon. Several brave passengers decided to take action and stop the hijackers. No one knows for sure exactly what happened, but it appears as though the passengers struggled with the terrorists. During the struggle, the plane careened out of control and dove into the ground in a field in Pennsylvania. All forty-five people on board died in the crash. The heroic efforts of the passengers, however, undoubtedly saved countless other lives.

The World Trade Center and the Pentagon were carefully chosen targets. The twin towers were not only two of the tallest skyscrapers in the world, they were also symbols of U.S. economic power. The Pentagon is not only one of the largest office buildings in the world, it's also a symbol of U.S. military power. Attacking the United States on its own soil was a way for the terrorists to show that the country was vulnerable. It was also a way to instill fear in Americans and their allies.

The September 11 attacks were most likely planned years in advance. All nineteen terrorists were originally from Middle Eastern countries but had been living in the United States. Investigators learned that several of them had taken flying lessons. They had trained to be commercial pilots so that they could take control of the hijacked jets and accurately fly them into their targets. The attacks

■ The Pentagon near Washington, D.C., smokes as flames engulf a section of the huge building after a hijacked jetliner crashed into it on the morning of September 11. Over 3,000 people died in the Al Qaeda–led attacks on New York City and Washington, D.C.

were well organized and executed by terrorists willing to die in the name of Allah. They were all members of Al Qaeda—Osama bin Laden's terrorist network.

Failed Attacks

Not all of Osama bin Laden's attacks on Americans have been successful. The U.S. government has been keeping track of bin Laden's activities for many years. Authorities received intelligence information before several planned attacks and were able to prevent them.

One of the largest foiled plots involved an attempt to bomb Los Angeles International Airport. The bombing was scheduled to occur during the millennium celebrations in the days before January 1, 2000. The Algerian man who pled guilty to charges of planning the attack said that he was trained at one of bin Laden's terrorist camps in Afghanistan. Other failed attacks included plots to assassinate President Bill Clinton and Pope John Paul II while they were visiting the Philippines. Osama bin Laden has also been linked to an assassination attempt against the president of Egypt.

America Strikes Back

Following the African embassy bombings, the United States made its first attempt at retaliation against Osama bin Laden. In August 1998, President Clinton ordered cruise missile strikes on targets associated with bin Laden. The targets were terrorist training camps in Afghanistan and a pharmaceutical plant in Sudan. The plant was thought to be manufacturing chemical weapons. These attacks, however, were unsuccessful. The terrorist training camps had

■ The El-Shifa pharmaceutical factory in Khartoum, Sudan, sits in ruins following a United States cruise missile attack on August 20, 1998. The bombing was in response to the African embassy attacks earlier that year. The Khartoum factory was allegedly making chemical weapons. Information learned later proved this was not true.

already been abandoned, and the pharmaceutical plant had not been used illegally.

After this failure, the United States attempted to keep bin Laden's activities in check. It used information from Arab intelligence agencies to thwart several planned attacks. The U.S. government also tried to get Pakistan, which had close ties with the Taliban, to pressure the group into turning over bin Laden. That attempt failed, however. The United States would make its most aggressive effort to find and eliminate bin Laden after the September 11 attacks on America.

CHAPTER FIVE

AMERICA'S MOST WANTED

■ President George W. Bush spoke to Americans after the terrorist attacks of September 11. He assured the public that America would find the perpetrators of the attacks. Within days, intelligence suspected Al Qaeda had masterminded the attacks.

On the evening of September 11, 2001, President George W. Bush addressed the nation. He called the attacks on the World Trade Center and the Pentagon "evil, despicable acts of terror." He vowed to use

President Bush meets with Defense Secretary Donald Rumsfeld, National Security Advisor Condoleeza Rice, and other officials at the Pentagon on September 17, 2001. Bush warned Americans that more casualties would come as the war on terrorism began.

national resources to "find those responsible and bring them to justice. We will make no distinction between the terrorists who committed these acts and those who harbor them."

Four days later, in his weekly radio address, President Bush outlined the country's response to the terrorist acts. "This will be a different kind of conflict against a different kind of enemy," he said. "This is a conflict without battlefields or beachheads, a conflict with opponents who believe they are invisible. Yet, they are mistaken." Bush went on to explain that this war would be a long one. "Victory against terrorism will not take place in a single battle, but in a series of decisive actions against terrorist organizations and those who harbor and support them."

In Search of bin Laden

Within the first few days following the September 11 terrorist attacks, people around the world came to know the name Osama bin Laden. It soon became clear that President Bush's pledge to "find those responsible" meant locating Osama bin Laden. The president's vow to "make no distinction between the terrorists . . . and those who harbor them" meant taking down the Taliban in Afghanistan.

From the beginning, bin Laden was the FBI's prime suspect. He hated the United States and had declared it a Muslim duty to kill Americans—military or civilian. He had been charged with planning several previous acts of terrorism against Americans. The September 11 terrorists had used Al Qaeda's signature tactics—simultaneous attacks involving lengthy preparation and precise coordination. Following September 11, 2001, Osama bin Laden became America's most wanted fugitive. A $25 million reward was offered for information leading to his capture.

Although the U.S. government had a clear idea where bin Laden was, it wouldn't be easy to capture him. Bin Laden wasn't living in a palatial mansion. He didn't work in a large government office in a major city. Most likely, he was hiding out in the mountains and caves of Afghanistan. This is a huge area filled with treacherous terrain. It was unfamiliar to the U.S. troops who would be conducting the search. To complicate matters even further, bin Laden was known to move to a new location every day or two to avoid detection. In addition, bin Laden lived as a guest of the Taliban in Afghanistan. The Taliban had protected and helped bin Laden stay hidden.

Launching an Attack

In the weeks following the September 11 attacks, President Bush demanded that the Taliban give up bin Laden. He also demanded that the group get rid of Al Qaeda's training camps and other operations in Afghanistan. The Taliban refused to meet President Bush's demands. On October 7, 2001—less than a month

■ Taliban forces are hit by American bombs in the village of Esferghich, Afghanistan, on November 3, 2001. Afghanistan became the first target of the U.S. military's response to the September 11 attacks. Osama bin Laden was now on the run.

after the September 11 terrorist attacks—the United States launched its own attack. It began a series of air strikes on Taliban targets in Afghanistan.

Fall of the Taliban

Although the U.S. government expected a long war, the Taliban regime fell in only two months. U.S. forces, with the help of the Northern Alliance (a group of Afghan groups opposed to the Taliban), defeated the Taliban and gained control of Afghanistan.

81

■ Afghan Northern Alliance troops travel down a road near Rabat, 30 miles (48 km) from Kabul. The Northern Alliance worked with the United States to defeat the Taliban army. Using Afghan fighters helped the United States win support from Afghans throughout the country.

One reason the Taliban was defeated so quickly was because it had established little loyalty among the Afghan people. Many citizens of Afghanistan were fed up with the Taliban's strict rules and harsh punishment. Although they are usually opposed to outside intervention, many Afghan people welcomed the help of the U.S. forces. They were happy to see the oppressive Taliban government defeated. As soon as the Taliban was driven from power, many Afghan people celebrated. They did things that had been forbidden under Taliban rule. Men shaved their beards, and women showed their faces. People played music, watched television, and even flew kites just for fun.

Although the Taliban was ousted from power, Osama bin Laden proved difficult to locate. U.S. officials believe that he most likely remains at large, probably hiding in the mountains between Afghanistan and Pakistan. Despite the Taliban's defeat, bin Laden's Al Qaeda terrorist network is still operational, as evidenced by attacks in Morocco and Saudi Arabia in mid-May 2003.

War with Iraq

In spring 2003, President Bush and the U.S. government switched their focus away from Osama bin Laden and Afghanistan. They turned their attention instead to another Middle Eastern country and its leader—Iraq and Saddam Hussein. U.S. forces had fought Hussein and his troops in the 1991 Persian Gulf War. Although the United States had defeated the Iraqi army, it had failed to oust the country's leader.

More than ten years after the Gulf War, Saddam Hussein was thought to be manufacturing weapons of

COUNTRY CAPSULE: Iraq

Capital

Baghdad

Total Area

168,754 square miles (437,071 sq km) (slightly more than twice the size of Idaho)

Border Countries

Iran, Kuwait, Saudi Arabia, Jordan, Syria, Turkey

Population

25.5 million

Religions

Shia Muslim 65 percent; Sunni Muslim 32 percent; other 3 percent

Languages

Arabic, Kurdish, Assyrian, Armenian

Literacy Rate

58 percent

Imports

Food, medicine

Exports

Crude oil

Natural Resources

Oil, natural gas, phosphates, sulfur

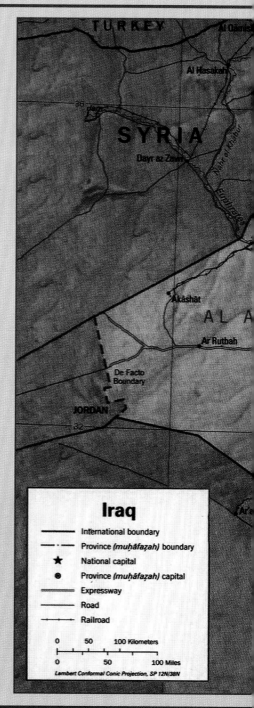

Iraq

— International boundary

— · — Province (muḥāfaẓah) boundary

★ National capital

◉ Province (muḥāfaẓah) capital

═══ Expressway

— Road

╁╁╁╁ Railroad

0   50   100 Kilometers

0   50   100 Miles

Lambert Conformal Conic Projection, SP 12N/38N

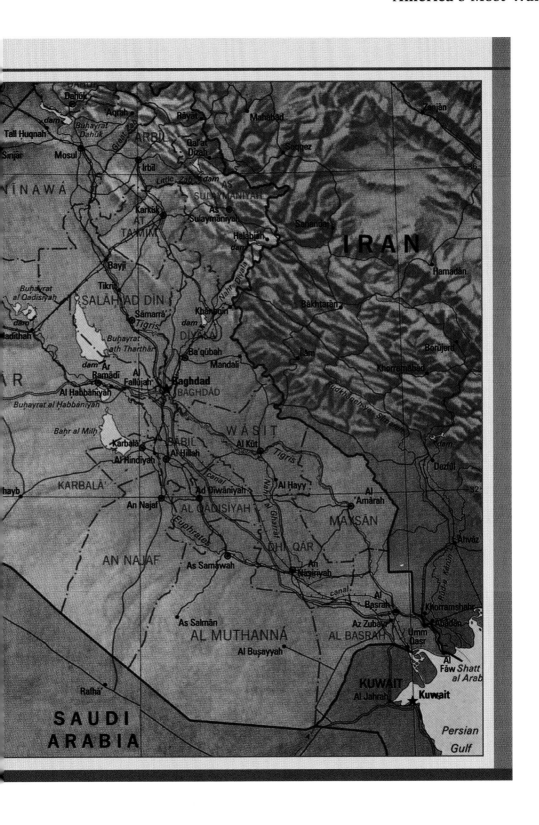

mass destruction. These chemical and biological weapons could kill thousands of people at one time. The governments of the United States and Great Britain decided that it was time to remove Saddam Hussein from power. The war with Iraq—known as Operation Iraqi Freedom—began on March 19, 2003, and practically ended on April 9, 2003, with the fall of Baghdad.

Bin Laden's Ties with Hussein

In the first days of the 2003 Iraq war, United States air forces dropped bombs on several key Iraqi targets. These targets were important political facilities for Saddam Hussein's regime. Sometime after the bombings, newspaper reporters began sifting through the rubble of the buildings. One of the buildings was the Iraqi intelligence headquarters.

According to an April 26, 2003, Associated Press article, reporters for the *Toronto Star* and Britain's *Sunday Telegraph* found several interesting documents within the rubble of the Iraqi intelligence headquarters. These documents appeared to link Saddam Hussein and Osama bin Laden. The documents showed that a meeting took place between members of Saddam Hussein's regime and an Al Qaeda representative in 1998. The purpose of the meeting seems to have been to start a relationship between the two groups. The relationship was based on their mutual hatred of the United States and the Saudi government. The papers also discussed arrangements for bin Laden to visit Baghdad and meet with Iraqi officials.

Osama bin Laden had never been a friend to Saddam Hussein before. This was proven by his public-spoken

■ Reports have circulated for many years that bin Laden and Hussein worked together in terrorist plots. No evidence to date has proven such a relationship. Bin Laden has publicly stated his hate for Hussein. These statements could someday be proved to be a smokescreen.

hatred for Hussein. Bin Laden thought Hussein was an infidel for not ruling Iraq by way of Islamic law. Hussein was a secular (nonreligious) ruler who used his Muslim religion when it suited his goals. Bin Laden, therefore, had publicly opposed Hussein. Nevertheless, the two leaders did have common interests—their hatred of the United States and their desire to rid the Middle East of U.S. military forces. The documents found after the U.S. bombing of Iraq, however, suggested that the two had come together. Experts had long suspected that there were ties between Saddam Hussein and Osama bin Laden. But until these documents were found, they had no real information that the Iraqi leader and Al Qaeda leader were linked.

Do these documents provide convincing proof of a bin Laden–Hussein connection? At the time of this book's writing, American intelligence services continue to investigate this question. So also do media sources. There have been several reports in the past that have brought up the claimed link between bin Laden and Hussein, dating back as far as 1999. These include *Newsweek* and *Time* magazine articles appearing on the same day, January 11, 1999. The two articles assert a connection between bin Laden's desire to use worldwide terror attacks to make Arab countries stop their backing of the United States with Hussein's desire to get those same Arab countries to break the embargo against Iraq. The connection was made by linking bin Laden's desires with Hussein's, though no real evidence was given to prove the articles' claims.

What this possible Saddam Hussein connection means to America's search for Osama bin Laden remains

■ The Al-Hamra compound in Saudi Arabia was one of several terrorist attacks happening simultaneously on May 13, 2002. The attacks proved that Al Qaeda was still active, despite claims by the Bush administration that members of the organization were on the run.

uncertain. In the meantime, the Bush administration, the CIA, and international intelligence agencies continue their search for the Al Qaeda leader.

Withdrawal of Troops

About 5,000 U.S. troops had been stationed in Saudi Arabia since the 1991 Persian Gulf War. The United States had used Saudi Arabia as a base of operations. When the war ended with the expelling of Iraqi troops from Kuwait, the U.S. troops stayed in Saudi Arabia. From there, they enforced a no-fly zone over southern Iraq.

With the start of the 2003 Iraq war, the number of U.S. troops in Saudi Arabia doubled from 5,000 to 10,000. A total of more than 250,000 American troops took part in the war effort. In less than two months, Operation Iraqi Freedom forced Saddam Hussein from power and the United States gained control of Iraq. After President Bush declared that the war was over, the United States decided to end military operations in Saudi Arabia. In a "mutual agreement" between the Saudi and U.S. governments, the United States removed nearly all of its troops from the region. The U.S. government planned to leave behind a small number of military personnel to train Saudi soldiers.

Experts agree that the decision to withdraw the U.S. troops should have a significant impact on America's relations with the Middle East. One of Osama bin Laden's biggest gripes with the United States was the stationing of troops in Saudi Arabia. So, the experts say, the withdrawal of these troops from Muslim Holy Land could help ease tensions between the United States and some Arab nations.

United States Secretary of State Colin Powell visited the bombed areas in Riyadh, Saudi Arabia. Since the May 2003 bombings, the United States has worked with the Saudi government to crack down on terrorist cells within Saudi Arabia. Investigations and arrests began to take place almost immediately.

Taped messages claiming to have been recorded by either Osama bin Laden or Dr. Ayman al-Zawahiri, Al Qaeda's second-in-command, continued to surface in 2003. The messages urged Muslims to attack American interests around the world. One of the tapes mentioned Saudi Arabia and Morocco as possible targets.

Riyadh Bombings

Soon after the Iraq war ended, it appeared as though Al Qaeda terrorists had struck again. On May 12, 2003,

■ Anti-American feelings still rage throughout much of the Muslim world. Here, Pakistani demonstrators in Multan, Pakistan, march against the start of America's war with Iraq. Today, it is believed that Osama bin Laden is still hiding in the mountains between Afghanistan and Pakistan.

car bombs exploded in the Saudi capital of Riyadh. By the time the dust had settled, thirty-four people, including nine Americans, had been killed in the blasts. About 200 other people were injured, including forty Americans.

The car bombs were detonated simultaneously at three foreign housing compounds in Riyadh. Nine suicide bombers first shot the security guards stationed in front of the buildings. Then they drove into the compounds and set off the explosives. The blasts were so powerful that the outer walls of four- and five-story buildings were blown out. President Bush condemned the bombings, saying, "These despicable acts were committed by killers whose only faith is hate . . ."

Although no terrorist organization immediately claimed responsibility, U.S. Secretary of State Colin Powell said that the attacks "had the finger-prints" of Al Qaeda. Many of Al Qaeda's previous attacks, including those of September 11, were similarly well planned and coordinated. Other Al Qaeda attacks, including the 1998 bombings of U.S. embassies in Africa, involved suicide car bombers.

Casablanca Bombings

Just five days after the Riyadh bombings, terrorists struck again. This time, five suicide bombers hit four separate targets in Casablanca, Morocco. Within twenty minutes, the terrorists had exploded bombs at a hotel, a restaurant, a social club, and a community center. In all, forty-one people were killed in the Casablanca bombings.

These attacks also looked very much like the work of Al Qaeda. The day after the bombings, authorities in Morocco took several Islamic militant suspects into custody and questioned them. A senior Moroccan official told *Time* magazine that the suspects had been "indoctrinated, trained, organized, and put into motion by foreign members of the international jihad movement." He then clarified, "We're talking about Al Qaeda here."

The Future of Terrorism

If the Riyadh bombings are linked to Al Qaeda, it would show that Osama bin Laden's terrorist network is still active. Does this also mean that Osama bin Laden is still alive? No one can say for sure. Many U.S. government officials thought that the military had killed bin Laden during the bombings in Afghanistan. Later, intelligence experts claimed bin Laden was most likely still alive. If the attacks in Riyadh and Casablanca were the usual well-planned attacks of Al Qaeda, more people will believe that bin Laden indeed still lives. And if bin Laden still controls Al Qaeda operations, then the world can be fairly certain that more terrorist attacks will come.

■ A police officer inspects the bomb damage at the Casa de Espana restaurant in Casablanca, Morocco. Multiple bombings in the city on May 17, 2003, killed at least forty people. Al Qaeda was behind these bombings. Its wrath now affects all who have relations with the United States.

Regardless of whether or not Osama bin Laden is still alive, however, most experts predict that Al Qaeda's terrorist attacks will continue. Just a few days before the Riyadh bombings, President Bush declared, "Nearly one-half of Al Qaeda's senior operatives have been captured or killed." Although that estimate is most likely accurate, many analysts feel that Al Qaeda remains a serious threat to the United States, its allies, and American interests worldwide.

"Definitely, [Al Qaeda's] capability has been eroded," a senior government official told the *New York*

Times. "But they are still a threat, they are still sophisticated, they are still fighting, and they are still trying to strike in the United States.

Osama bin Laden's Legacy

For most Americans, the terrorist attacks of September 11, 2001, were a wake-up call. The United States had not seen a great deal of terrorism on its own soil. Americans had grown used to going about their everyday lives without much worry about their safety.

After September 11, the United States—and the world—became a different place. Americans discovered that there were people who hated the United States and everything it stood for. Americans found out that their country was more susceptible to attack than they had once imagined. They also realized that events that take place on the other side of the world could have serious consequences at home.

America's Response

So how has the United States responded to the September 11 terrorist attacks? Security has been tightened around the country, especially at airports and borders. President Bush announced the creation of the Department of Homeland Security—a new government agency designed to help protect the country from terrorism. And many average American citizens responded by paying closer attention to their surroundings.

For Osama bin Laden, America's response to the events of September 11 was probably not the reaction he had expected or hoped to provoke. As with all acts of terrorism, the September 11 attacks were intended to instill

■ Al Qaeda leader Osama bin Laden is seen in this image made from television aired by the Arabic satellite channel Al-Jazeera on Wednesday, September 10, 2003. The tape was said to have been made five months earlier. Despite Bush administration statements claiming bin Laden and Al Qaeda are "on the run," this videotape and recent bombings around the world suggest the terrorist and his organization remain active.

great fear. Shortly after the attacks, bin Laden declared, "America will never dream nor those who live in America will never taste security and safety . . ." Although many Americans are more cautious now than they once were, most have not let fear rule their lives. Osama bin Laden did not win his war of terrorism with the United States.

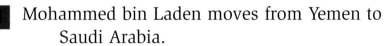

1931 Mohammed bin Laden moves from Yemen to Saudi Arabia.

1957 Osama bin Laden, the seventeenth son of Mohammed bin Laden, is born in Saudi Arabia.

1967 Mohammed bin Laden is killed in a plane crash. His son Osama inherits an estimated $250 million.

1974 At the age of seventeen, Osama bin Laden marries his first wife.

1979 Osama bin Laden graduates from King Abdul Aziz University with a degree in management and economics.

December 26: The Soviet Union invades Afghanistan. Bin Laden volunteers to join the fight against the Soviets.

1989 Soviet troops finally leave Afghanistan, ending a ten-year war.

1990 August 2: Iraq invades Kuwait, leading to the first Persian Gulf War.

1991 Bin Laden is expelled from Saudi Arabia. He moves to Sudan and establishes the Al Qaeda terrorist headquarters.

1993 February 26: A bomb explodes in the parking garage of the World Trade Center in New York City. The convicted mastermind of the attack, Ramzi Yousef, has ties to Osama bin Laden.

October 3: Eighteen American servicemen are killed in Somalia. Bin Laden is charged with

training the guerrillas who took part in
the attack.

1994 Saudi Arabia revokes Osama bin Laden's
citizenship, and his family disowns him.

1996 Under pressure from the United States and Saudi
Arabia, bin Laden is expelled from Sudan.
He returns to Afghanistan, where the Taliban
has become the ruling government.

August 23: Bin Laden issues his first fatwa
against Americans and Jews in the Holy
Land, calling for strikes against U.S.
troops in the Persian Gulf.

1998 February: Bin Laden issues his second fatwa
against the United States, calling for the
death of all Americans.

August 7: Two truck bombs explode outside U.S.
embassies in Kenya and Tanzania in Africa.
The U.S. government charges bin Laden with
the bombings.

August 20: President Bill Clinton orders cruise
missile strikes on targets associated with
bin Laden.

1999 Osama bin Laden is added to the FBI's list of
Ten Most Wanted Fugitives.

2000 Osama bin Laden marries his fourth wife.

October 12: Suicide bombers detonate explosives
next to the U.S. Navy battleship USS *Cole*,
docked at the port of Aden in Yemen. The
suspects accused of planning the attack were
trained in bin Laden's terrorist camps.

2001 September 11: Terrorists hijack four American jetliners, crashing two into the World Trade Center, one into the Pentagon, and one into a field in Pennsylvania. All of the hijackers were members of Osama bin Laden's Al Qaeda network.

October 7: The United States begins a series of air strikes on Taliban targets in Afghanistan.

December 9: The Taliban government is defeated and driven from power.

2003 March 20: The U.S. and British governments begin a war with Iraq, known as Operation Iraqi Freedom.

May 1: President George W. Bush declares the end of major combat operations in Iraq.

May 12: Car bombs explode in Riyadh, Saudi Arabia. The explosions are thought to be the work of Al Qaeda.

September 10: A videotape showing bin Laden walking in the mountains of what purportedly is the Pakistan-Afghanistan border region is released by the Arabic satellite channel Al-Jazeera. The tape was said to have been made in April or May of 2003.

GLOSSARY

Allah The name of God in Islam.

Al Qaeda Arabic word meaning "the base"; a network of terrorists organized by Osama bin Laden.

assassinate To murder someone by sudden or secret attack.

cell A small unit of an organization or movement.

Communism A government system in which all property is collectively owned.

dissident A person who disagrees with an established government or organization.

embassy The official home and offices of an ambassador to a foreign country.

execution A putting to death, especially as punishment for a crime.

exile A person who has been forced to leave his or her country or home.

fatwa A religious decree from an Islamic leader.

fundamentalist A person who follows a movement that emphasizes strict obedience to a set of principles or beliefs.

guerrilla Having to do with unconventional warfare. A guerrilla is a person who takes part in such warfare as part of an independent group.

hijack To forcefully take over the controls of an airplane in flight.

infidel A nonbeliever, or person who does not follow a particular religion.

Islam The religious faith of Muslims.

jihad A holy war waged in the name of Islam.

Koran The holy book of Islam.

mosque An Islamic house of worship.

mujahideen "Holy warriors" who fought against the Soviet Union during its invasion of Afghanistan.

mullah A title of respect for a Muslim who is educated in traditional religious law and holds an official post.

Muslim One who believes in Islam.

Taliban "Religious students" in Arabic; a group of Muslim fundamentalists that ruled Afghanistan from 1996 to 2001.

terrorism The use of violence to threaten or hurt people in an attempt to achieve political goals.

FOR MORE INFORMATION

Organizations

Amnesty International (U.S. office)
322 8th Avenue
New York, NY 10001
(212) 807-8400
e-mail: admin-us@aiusa.org
Web site: http://www.amnestyusa.org

Anti-Defamation League (ADL)
823 United Nations Plaza
New York, NY 10017
Web site: http://www.adl.org

The Arab Organization for Human Rights (AOHR)
91 Al-Marghany Street
Heliopolis, Cairo, Egypt
e-mail: aohr@link.com.eg

Council on American-Islamic Relations
453 New Jersey Avenue SE
Washington, DC 20003
Web site: http://www.cair-net.org

Federal Bureau of Investigation (FBI)
J. Edgar Hoover Building
935 Pennsylvania Avenue NW
Washington, DC 20535-0001
Web site: http://www.fbi.gov

Middle East Studies Association of North America
c/o The University of Arizona
1643 E. Helen Street
(520) 621-5850
e-mail: mesana@u.arizona.edu
Web site: http://w3fp.arizona.edu/mesassoc

National Council on U.S.-Arab Relations
1140 Connecticut Avenue NW, Suite 1210
Washington, DC 20036
Web site: http://www.ncusar.org

United States Department of Homeland Security
Washington, DC 20528
Web site: http://www.dhs.gov

United States Department of State
2201 C Street NW
Washington, DC 20520
(202) 647-4000
Web site: http://www.state.gov

Women's Commission for Refugee Women & Children
122 East 42nd Street
New York, NY 10168
(212) 551-3111 or (212) 551-3088
e-mail: wcrwc@womenscommission.org

Web Sites

Due to the changing nature of Internet links, the Rosen Publishing Group, Inc., has developed an online list of Web sites related to the subject of this book. This site is updated regularly. Please use this link to access the list:

http://www.rosenlinks.com/mel/obla

FOR FURTHER READING

Frank, Mitch. *Understanding September 11th: Answering Questions About the Attacks on America.* New York: Viking, 2002.

Gard, Carolyn. *The Attacks on the World Trade Center: February 26, 1993, and September 11, 2001.* New York: Rosen Publishing Group, 2003.

Lalley, Patrick. *9.11.01: Terrorists Attack the U.S.* Austin, TX: Raintree/Steck-Vaughn, 2002.

Landau, Elaine. *Osama bin Laden: A War Against the West.* Brookfield, CT: Twenty-First Century Books, 2002.

Loehfelm, Bill. *Osama bin Laden* (Heroes & Villains). San Diego: Lucent Books, 2003.

Louis, Nancy. *Osama bin Laden* (War on Terrorism). Edina, MN: Abdo & Daughters, 2002.

Wheeler, Jill C. *September 11, 2001: The Day That Changed America* (War on Terrorism). Edina, MN: Abdo & Daughters, 2002.

Woolf, Alex. *Osama bin Laden.* Minneapolis: Lerner Publications, 2003.

BIBLIOGRAPHY

Biography.com. "Osama bin Laden." Retrieved
    January 24, 2003 (http://search.biography.com/
    print_record.pl?id = 23987).

CNN.com. "Bin Laden, Millionaire with a Dangerous
    Grudge." Retrieved February 21, 2003
    (http://www.cnn.com/2001/US/09/12/
    binladen.profile).

Dobbs, Michael. "Inside the Mind of Osama Bin
    Laden." *Washington Post*, September 20, 2001,
    page A01.

Elliott, Michael. "Why the War on Terror Will Never
    End." *Time*, May 26, 2003, p. 26.

Frank, Mitch. *Understanding September 11th:
    Answering Questions About the Attacks on
    America*. New York: Viking, 2002.

Frank, Mitch. "A Wealthy Clan and Its Renegade."
    Time, October 8, 2001, page 63.

Hayes, Laura. "Al-Qaeda: Osama bin Laden's Network
    of Terror." Infoplease.com. Retrieved January 24,
    2003 (http://www.infoplease.com/spot/
    terror-qaeda.html).

Hayes, Laura. "Who Are the Taliban?" Infoplease.com.
    Retrieved January 24, 2003 (http://www.
    infoplease.com/spot/taliban.html).

Johnson, David. "Who Is Osama bin Laden?"
    Infoplease.com. Retrieved January 24, 2003
    (http://www.infoplease.com/spot/
    osamabinladen.html).

Louis, Nancy. *Osama bin Laden* (War on Terrorism).
    Edina, MN: Abdo & Daughters, 2002.

"Meet the bin Ladens." *Newsweek*, October 15,
   2001, p. 55.
Satchell, Michael. "The Making of a Terrorist." *U.S.
   News and World Report*, October 12, 2001, p. 40.
Smith, Patricia. "America's Most Wanted." *New York
   Times Upfront*, October 15, 2001, p. 14.
Vilbig, Peter. "Why Do They Hate America?" *New York
   Times Upfront*, October 15, 2001, p. 10.

INDEX

About the Author

Suzanne J. Murdico is a freelance writer who has authored numerous books for children and teens. She lives near Tampa, Florida, with her husband, Vinnie, and their cat, Zazu.

Photo Credits

Cover, pp. 3 (chapter 1 box), 12–13, 24–25, 30–31, 56–57, 84–85 © Perry-Castãnedia Library Map Collection/The University of Texas at Austin; cover image, pp. 1, 3 (chapter 4 and 5 boxes), 6, 26–27, 49, 52, 66–67, 74–75, 87, 91, 97 © AP/Wide World Photos; pp. 3 (chapter 2 box), 33, 34, 65 © Sayyid Azim/AP/ Wide World Photos; pp. 3 (chapter 3 box), 42–43 © Haidar Shah/AP/Wide World Photos; pp. 4, 8, 16–17, 41, 50 © Corbis; pp. 14–15, 18–19, 29, 38–39, 61 © Reuters New Media Inc./ Corbis; p. 22 © Liu Heung Shing/AP/Wide World Photos; p. 36 © Reza/Webistan/Corbis; p. 44 © Tim Johnston/AP/Wide World Photos; p. 46–47 © Santiago Lyon/AP/Wide World Photos; p. 54–55 © John Moore/AP/Wide World Photos; p. 59 © Eyal Warshavsky/AP/Wide World Photos; pp. 62–63 © Richard Drew/ AP/Wide World Photos; p. 70–71 © Jerry Torrens/AP/Wide World Photos; p. 73 © Heesoon Yim/AP/Wide World Photos; pp. 77, 78–79 © Doug Mills/AP/Wide World Photos; pp. 81, 82 © Marco Di Lauro/AP/Wide World Photos; p. 88–89 © Ali Fraidoon/ AP/Wide World Photos; p. 92–93 © Khalid Tanveer/AP/Wide World Photos; p. 95 © Denis Doyle/AP/Wide World Photos.

Designer: Nelson Sá; **Editor:** Mark Beyer
Photo Researcher: Nelson Sá